African-American

—Christian   Isolation

African-Canadian

HYPHENATED

———

WHY

?

Exclusiveness   Isolation

African-American

—Christian   Isolation

African-Canadian

HYPHENATED

———

WHY

?

Exclusiveness Isolation

Robert C. Hollingsworth

To order additional copies of this book, contact:
Xlibris Corporation
1-888-795-4274
www.Xlibris.com
Orders@Xlibris.com
60034

This exploration of human relations
is dedicated to the purpose of
'coming-along-side' to help alleviate
the pain associated with isolation.

CONTENTS

FOUNDATIONAL
THOUGHT

~~~~~~~~~~~~~~~~

FOUNDATIONAL THOUGHT

I am intrigued with relational dynamics displayed in our society and magnified by the media. Electoral results in the United States, have certainly received our attention. President Obama when interviewed on 60 Minutes, successfully side-stepped making reference to 'race' during the election. I applauded Mr. Obama and was very thankful for the position he took during his interview.

There are (it goes without saying) obvious differences that do not require examination. Differences are extremely clear. I remember quite well a situation when an acquaintance was in conversation with someone who did not know me. The conversation ended with the unknown person saying to my acquaintance; "He is a man of colour, you know". My acquaintance responded; "He is?"

This reference indicates two possible responses that are common in human relationships. Was the response by the person who knew me, a sarcastic response? Of course he knew I am a person of colour.

On the other hand, was this response an indication that the colour of my skin was of no consequence?

Having been raised in a country and in a home that stressed individualism, I have been able to maintain a position of acceptance or rejection, on my own merits. I have been spared the malady of 'wearing my colour on my sleeve'. Not everything negative that takes place relationally is because of my colour. I may not have been accepted for the job because someone was more qualified than I was. I was not able to rent that apartment because someone else had been there before me. When I was living with my parents, we were never refused accommodation anywhere my parents had applied. Since becoming married and having a family of my own, we have never been refused accommodation wherever we have applied.

In my working experience, I have never been turned down for a job because of the colour of my skin.

I have held a number of significant positions during my working experience. The work ethic I have been able to develop and carry out has served me well. I have to state as well, that I have not been spared from incidents of 'racial putdowns', but I have been able to attribute those isolated incidents to expressions of ignorance.

Throughout my journey of life I have had amazing opportunities to experience interaction with whomever, regardless of the colour of their skin. Now that I have reached retirement and the stage in my life where it is acceptable for me to compare relational developments, I am troubled and to some degree confused by relational developments taking place. Having received theological training in the United States at the height of the Civil Rights movement, I was introduced to relational dynamics I had not experienced before.

As well as rooming in a dormitory with three students for the first time in my life, I was introduced to new relational struggles. Students of colour from the southern states found my interaction with whomever, difficult to accept. I did not isolate myself, but extended myself to whomever I desired to make contact with rather successfully. The Bible school was located in one of the northern states and was, for all intents and purposes, a 'safe' location.

I did, however, encounter for the first time in my 18 years blatant discrimination. My father had always cut my hair. Even though he had his hair cut in a local barbershop, he chose to cut his sons' hair. Perhaps it was from an economical need. In any case, here I was over 500 miles from home needing a haircut. What was I to do? I couldn't very well drive home to get my hair cut. I had to go to a barbershop. When I found a barbershop in the vicinity of the school I had to wait my turn. As I sat in the shop my turn came to sit in the barber's chair. I waited for the invitation to move forward from where I was sitting, but the invitation did not come. Instead, I was escorted outside and the barber pointed up the street to where I could get my hair cut.

I walked in the direction he pointed. I never found the shop he supposedly pointed to. It was made clear to me when I returned to campus, that I would have to go into the 'coloured section' of the city to get my hair cut. I thought to myself, "Welcome to the United States of America".

My three years in this environment, was an education in many ways. Following graduation, I returned to my home in Ontario, Canada with a clearer understanding of the struggle many people of colour experience relationally. I continue to be very thankful and appreciative of the life I have been able to enjoy in Canada.

For fear of presenting Canada as the epitome of human relationships, I do have concerns as to what is taking place even in this 'glorious and free' land. There is a definite change in relational dynamics in the community of the people of colour. I realize my usage of the term 'people of colour' is an antiquated term that has been replaced by the term 'black'. This is a throw-back to the days of my youth. There are many changes taking place and I would have to say, not all these changes are positive as it relates to human relations.

There was a time when you would meet a fellow person of colour and there would be an acknowledgement that you were there. There would be a smile or some acknowledgement. There was never anything written that was to take place; it just happened. Today, however, your path may cross with that of a person of the visible minority, and there is no recognition. It would seem that you are 'making out' with that person instead of just acknowledging you are in the same ethnic camp. This may appear insignificant, but to my mind it is indicative of changing dynamics even within the community of the people of colour.

There is, however, a more significant and troubling dynamic that is having a negative effect on human relations. What is currently taking place is heightened reference to ethnic origin.
No longer is a person of colour Canadian or American. They are African-Canadian or African-American. I question the value and purpose of this hyphenated term. Comments have been made to justify the usage of the term to highlight ethnic origin. My ancestors were from Africa. I am therefore an African-Canadian. The same hold true for that person residing in the United States. "My ancestors were from Africa. I am therefore an African-American".
I have heard comments that attempt to explain this hyphenated usage. It is to help ensure one does not lose sight of their 'roots'. And in the same way, others will recognize where we are from ethnically. I may be missing something here, but I don't think there is need for me to make a statement that my ancestors were from Africa. I didn't get this dark complexion from cosmetics. It is not my intent to

appear sarcastic, but I question how this designation serves to enhance positive human relations.

As far as this 'label' being used to assist personal identity of origin, I question the role of parents in this regard. If a youngster questions where they are from, can the parent not sit down and rehearse the ethnic progression with them?

When accessing a web page that dealt with hyphenated usage, a comment stated that this practice creates inability to be a melting pot. It serves to heighten differences instead of creating opportunity to diminish them. Webster's Encyclopedic Dictionary gives the definition of a melting pot as being that which races and cultures mingle to form a whole. The comment from the web page stating that usage of the hyphenated term creates the inability to be a melting pot would indicate a reluctance to mingle and form a whole.

Reluctance to mingle and work at becoming a 'whole' results in a grouping together with those of like passions and purposes. This outcome has become very evident as of late. The ghetto mentality and presence has become very real and frightening to the general population. While it may be true that to mingle and group with those of similar goals and aspirations could provide a sense of security, there are negative results that outweigh any possible benefit from an isolated mentality.

It continues to be very intriguing to witness the creativity evident in the communities that have chosen to isolate themselves. Styles of clothing and communication have come to the forefront and have certainly with no hesitation, had an impact. It is to the point where reference to a thesaurus is required in order to communicate with those choosing isolation. This isolation mentality is rapidly creating a slippery slop resulting in further separation and isolation. We don't know each other and walls are being built to separate and keep those who are not of the same mind, beyond arm's length. I don't recall who composed the song that states; "No man is an island. No man stands alone. Each man as my brother. Each man as my friend". It would be of benefit if this song was resurrected and its meaning highlighted in our society by actions taken by all sides of the debate.

When witnessing isolationism, two questions come to mind. 1. What is the origin of this isolation mentality? 2. What

impact is it having on those who are not
advocates of this thinking?
I have lived in Canada all my life, with
the exception of when I received my
theological training. Throughout my life
there has never been any occasion when I
have felt as though I had to hide or amplify
my heritage. This was the common position
held by those who originally made Canada
their home.

Emphasis on ethnic origin became an
issue beginning in the late '70's. In a major
Ontario city, prior to this period, there
were no areas set aside to house those of
the same ethnic origin. We, whose skin is
darker than the majority of citizens in that
metropolitan city, were able to identify
with the city and enter into the fabric of
our homeland. We regarded ourselves as
citizens in the fullest sense of the word.
We were actually encouraged to take active
roles and positions where we could make
a difference. This was Canada. This was
what Canada was, and is all about.

I don't foresee Canada changing its role of
accepting those who want to make Canada
their home. I state very clearly, and without
hesitation, that Canada should continue to
be upheld and regarded as a great country

that accepts without bias, those wanting to make Canada their home. I would suggest that the issue of isolation has its origin from those who come to Canada, and do not identify with this country. It is as though in their minds, there is a re-location of their place of birth, but Canada is **NOT** Africa or any other country.

When an attempt is made to fashion a new place of residence according to what took place in the country of origin, problems surface that we are seeing now. Questions have to be asked to these new arrivals; "Why did you leave your homeland?" "Why are you living in Canada?" "What has Canada to offer that your homeland did not offer?"
Unfortunately, there are occasions when the same conflict that has been experienced elsewhere becomes the same conflict in their new homeland called Canada.

I had opportunity to read a book written by Martin Gilbert entitled, Churchill—Churchill and the Jews. He states that when members of that nation were persecuted and driven from their homeland, they sought refuge in countries that would accept them. When they were able to relocate, they identified with that country. They would enter

into its national life and while adhering faithfully to their own religion, would regard themselves as citizens in the fullest sense of the state which had received them. (Churchill and the Jews: A Lifelong Friendship. McClelland & Stewart) There was no isolation mentality.
Members of that nation sought to make a contribution to their new homeland. They did not forsake their roots, but sought to mingle in order to form a whole in their new homeland.

I have often viewed scenes of Africa with its vast beauty and wished that I were able to visit. Large amounts of money continue to be spent in tracking lineage. I have been told, to some degree, my heritage but it is very limited. I do know there was some involvement concerning the Underground Railroad but, to what extent, I'm not too clear. I don't know if my roots have their origin in Africa or Ethiopia. There is no doubt that my roots go beyond Canada, but Canada is my home. I have a responsibility to make a contribution to my homeland. I am Canadian, eh!

Another question came to mind as I developed this exploration. What impact is this isolation mentality having on us who do not subscribe and are not advocates of this mentality? A supposition rears its ugly head as it relates to law enforcement. Unfortunately, we are seeing an increase in the number of those convicted of law offenses within the community of the people of colour. I am saddened when I see programs that *would appear* to highlight the number of black law breakers. News reports of how many people of colour are shooting each other continue to increase. What impact does this isolation mentality have on the rest of us? The supposition is that we are one of them, and the public has to be careful for fear of being shot. It is becoming 'easy' for the general population to engage in group mentality. It is therefore incumbent for us who desire to position ourselves in order to make a contribution, to work to accent the positive.

This aspect and practice of isolation is being observed in every segment of life; from habitation to social activities and to centers of education. Much attention has been given to the high percentage of 'dropouts' from the education system by those of the community of colour. Statistics have been gathered that indicate high numbers of students not finishing or graduating from high school, or not continuing their education beyond elementary schools. Various reasons have been given for this decline. One reason that has received the greatest attention is the lack of interest in the subject matter being taught. It has been suggested aggressively that the creation of a school whose mandate would be to teach subjects of ethnicity would ensure enrollment being maintained.

Afro-centrism is being advocated and pursued vigorously, with a school being prepared to open in a metropolitan city in Ontario. This would be the first such school in Canada.

Robert H. Bork in his book, Slouching Towards Gomorrah, states; "The programs taught in such schools tend to be indoctrination rather than education. The presence of Afro-centrism lowers scholarly standards generally". (Slouching Towards Gomorrah—Regan Books)

To create another isolated setting would do nothing but exacerbate an already serious situation as it relates to difficulty in developing and improving human relations. Attendance in such an isolated setting would not encourage positive relations beyond the confines of the school. Once again, interaction would take place within the groups of those attending the school.

Reviewing the approach educators are presently taking poses the question; How are students of colour who have emigrated, being prepared to take positions of influence when they are not being taught subjects that deal with the history and make-up of their new homeland?

In earlier times, Canada was set aside and looked upon as a country that presented a new and worthwhile climate for change. Those who immigrated to Canada formed a 'melting pot' in order to make a whole, a country offering a level of freedom not shared by any other country. Canada offered to those relocating an opportunity to contribute to the well being and good of each other. This is one of the reasons why many continue to migrate to Canada.

I would be remiss if I failed to make reference to a most importance aspect of influence in the make-up of Canada. I continue to be impressed, when I have opportunity to watch a National Hockey League game on television. Just before the teams make their way on to the ice an announcement is made. "Please stand and, gentlemen, remove your hats for the singing of the National Anthem". The cameras are focused on the one who is to sing the anthem. When the game is being played in Quebec, the anthem is sung in French. When outside of Quebec, the anthem is sung in English. Whether in French or English, when the words reach the point of the prayer contained in the anthem I have always heard the prayer sung in English. "God keep our land, glorious and free". At this point in the anthem, reference is made to the fact that God can be counted on to work at keeping this land glorious and free. There is entwined in the very fabric of this great and glorious land reference to our dependency of God to keep what He has created and allowed us to enjoy. Even though this ingrained and foundational ingredient in the make-up of Canada continues to be under attack, reference to dependency on the Creator, continues to be made. Suggestions have been made by those in positions of influence and power, to minimize and even eliminate reference to the Creator. Unfortunately, as a result, Canada is being called, not a Christian nation, but a secular nation. The nation south of us continues to be regarded as a Christian nation.

Many distinctions are 'part and parcel' of what is brought to a new location. We do not lose what made us who we are before we emigrated. This refers to tribal distinctive and cultural practices. What are we to do with that which is part of us as we settled into a new location? I suggest that this presents another distinction that separates us of the community of colour, from other 'groups' coming to Canada. We have no common language or custom that is common to everyone who has emigrated from Africa. Perhaps this could be a driving force towards the establishment of an Africentric school. Once again, how would this enhance relationships beyond those attending? How would this help new Canadians become familiar with what makes Canada unique? How would this assist new Canadians to enter into the 'melting pot'?

Is it possible that that which we have brought with us; that is part and parcel of what we are, can still be held, but within our own environment or homes? The pursuit of ethnic progression can still be addressed within the family framework. Is it possible that the breakdown of the family unit is forcing the need for societal support? Is it also possible that the absence of the male influence is adding to stress in the lives of young people? How difficult it must be for a single parent (usually a mother) who has to provide for her children, and be involved in other aspects of family life, to become engaged in making a contribution to her new homeland. Those facing these difficulties and continue to make a contribution are to be congratulated.

We are witnessing greater dependency on service and community groups that provide support through mentoring programs to address the absence of parental influence. Such programs are very visible in communities, and are proving to be instrumental in giving young people positive options. It is hoped that the positive climate provided for young people through these mentoring programs will result in young people seeking to make a contribution to the common good. Every effort must be made to assist with integration. I read, recently, of the creation of a unique communication group. The purpose of this group is to help immigrants develop communication skills, to learn how to speak. I was so impressed with this effort, that I made contact with the group leader expressing my appreciation. Incidentally, this group is meeting in the same city that has been targeted for the possible creation of an Africentric school. I made reference to the importance of embracing and understanding the foundation upon which Canada was built. The cry continues for God to keep this land glorious and free. It is imperative therefore, that barriers separating and leading to isolation be addressed and broken down.

When watching the news on a Canadian station (C.B.C. news, 28/01/09) the decision of the principal of an elementary school in a Maritime province to discontinue the singing of the National anthem that was part of the morning ritual was reported. This decision was made in response to concerns from other parents. Needless to say, there has been an overwhelming response both pro and con to this decision. Is this another indication of isolation or merely rebellion?

This isolation mentality is being found beyond the 'black' community. It appears however, that the black community has received greater media coverage than other groups who have immigrated to Canada. Other groups appear to be reluctant to incorporate the hyphen before their new homeland. Having said that, the presence and intent to remain independent and isolated from striving to mingle and work at 'making the whole' is evident when the attempt is made to transplant 'religious ideology'.

It is interesting to note the position taken in the homeland of those who strive to make their religious preference felt in their new homeland. According to reports from those who have investigated religious practices beyond the 'western world', religious segregation is very active. You must adhere to the major religious influence, or face horrendous persecution. When resettlement takes place in this land that is accepting and unbiased, there is evidence that intolerance found in the 'homeland' is being transferred and imported to the new homeland.

I have made reference to the news report regarding the decision to discontinue the singing of the Canadian National Anthem. This decision was based on the discomfort some parents experienced with their children having to sing the anthem. The birthplace of these parents was not disclosed during the initial report. I would dare say we have not heard the last of this issue. One comment that was received stated that the reason the parents were upset was because of the reference to God. It was further stated that the next thing to get changed will be the removal of God from our national anthem.

(Since making reference to this decision, the issue was brought to the Canadian House of Commons, where the school was ordered to begin playing the national anthem again—The Toronto Star—31/01/09)

The choice was made by these newcomers, to immigrate to this land and build lives and raise families on the foundation that had been created by those who came before. In the earlier days there was great emphasis on working to develop the whole, and be part of the melting pot. Appreciation was voiced emphatically for the opportunity to come to a land where they were accepted as people of worth and substance. Welcome to the land of the free.

~~~~~~~~~~~~~~~~~~~~

NOTES

COMMUNITY
OF FAITH

~~~~~~~~~~~~~~~~

COMMUNITY OF FAITH

The community of faith has not been spared from the effects of the isolation mentality. Church leaders find themselves confronted by those suffering from isolation even within their own congregations. The isolation experienced by those within the community of faith, has a different overtone than observed from those who have simply immigrated. Even though a different association is realized, the outward result of isolation occurs. Due to the insidiousness of this mentality within the community of faith, identification is difficult, with the result being, entrenchment.

The community of faith has been designated and assigned by God to provide a 'safe haven' for those who struggle with issues of life. It is in this environment that we are to find solace and support without incrimination, where we can 'bare our souls' with abandonment. We have been encouraged to feel 'safe' within the community of faith, based on the directive given in scripture as to how we are to treat each other. A high standard has been advocated and presented as a model to follow.

Unfortunately, when the 'guard' has been let down and a description has been given of internal struggles, is when some have experienced the greatest disappointment. When others have been invited to become partners with private issues and have used that information to belittle or judge, a negative outcome has been experienced. As a result of that negative experience, a wall of protection has been built, behind which those who have been hurt can hide. These walls provide isolation. In this regard, isolation is formed under a spiritual umbrella rather than an immigration umbrella. Regardless of the source, the outcome is the same. We are kept at arm's length from each other which results in isolation. The following scenario may prove to be helpful in describing this dilemma.

There was so much tension in the room that you could proverbially cut it with a knife. Throughout the ordeal, there was what could be described, as a 'knock-down-drag-out' attempt to do the other person in. Looking on, one would wonder where and when is this going to end? This is not the first time these two combatants have engaged in warfare, but this encounter seemed to have taken on a deeper and more intense focus than had been witnessed before.

Points of view were given to justify the approach each took in this regard. Reasons were given for the 'putdown'. The reaction to the putdown was also given.

When it seemed as though there was never going to be an end to this battle, a statement of sorrow was heard. "I am sorry I hurt you, will you forgive me?" A response following the request was heard as well. "Yes, I forgive you". All became quiet on the 'western front'. Well, not exactly.

As we were given opportunity to accompany the combatants as they maintained their daily routine, an examination of the previous encounter was made. An outcome to this encounter was also noticed.

The one, who had asked to be forgiven, stated they did not feel forgiven. The one who supposedly granted the request to forgive was overheard stating that, even though they had forgiven, they could not forget. There were two distinct actions, with two distinct outcomes. One asked forgiveness, but did not feel forgiven. The other was to give forgiveness, but could not/would not forget the reason why forgiveness was asked.

When examining this scenario, a number of questions come to mind. When seeking forgiveness, should we seek to 'feel' forgiveness? What is this feeling of forgiveness? When granting forgiveness, how important is it to forget the reason for granting forgiveness? Is it necessary to forget? What is the outcome if forgetfulness does not accompany forgiveness? How do we go about forgetting? Is it possible to forget?

Forgiveness is placed on a high level of importance. Members of the family of faith are admonished throughout scripture to engage in the act and practice of forgiveness. To forgive is to pardon, to excuse a wrong or a wrongdoer. (Webster's Encyclopedic Dictionary)

To seek forgiveness is to acknowledge that you have done something wrong to someone. You have done something other than what you would want that person to do to you. To seek forgiveness forces you to pull down the veil of outward perfection to reveal the truth of your imperfection. For you to ask forgiveness is to show compassion and concern about the possible deterioration of a relationship. Much regret accompanies this admission.

What directive have we been given in addressing and following through in this practice? Jesus gave the directive as found in the Gospel of Matthew 5:23, 24. "If you are offering your gift at the alter and there remember that your brother (sister—added) has **something against you** (emphasis added) leave your gift there before the alter and go; first be reconciled to your brother (sister-added) and then come and offer your gift. (Revised Standard Version, R.S.V.)
With this directive, Jesus is telling us that we are **not** to wait until the brother or sister who has something against us comes to us. We are to go to them. Even though this directive does not specifically address the act of asking forgiveness, it does give clear direction to the start of the healing process by one going and being reconciled.

This reveals the reality of a person being transparent and sensitive. There are times when you sense something is wrong in a relationship and you feel compelled to investigate. Upon investigation, you discover the need to be forgiven.

Once again, the process of healing begins when you go to that person who you sensed had a problem in the relationship. Whatever position you take at this point, the first step is simply to ask forgiveness. You have discharged your personal obligation and asked forgiveness. You have put your own feelings 'on the line'.

When pursuing the initial steps in the healing of a relationship that has gone awry, there are other considerations to be taken into account. These considerations are often referenced as to why we do not follow through in obedience to the Divine directive. However, any consideration that may be referenced cannot justify downright disobedience to the directive given by our Saviour.

"What if I ask forgiveness, and they won't forgive me?" "I will only make matters worst if I make contact, and there is nothing going on". These and other considerations may be justified as far as they go, but when the root cause of these comments are examined, it will be discovered that they have more to do with our pride than with anything else. Is it possible that the

Spirit of God brought the issue to your mind so that you could come-along-side to reinforce the relationship you should have with your brother or sister? If there has been no effort in the investigation of a possible rift in the relationship, how will closure occur? What will be the result if closure does not occur?

There are occasions in life, when we can just let things slide. However, as it relates to relationships, this does not apply if we are intent on following the directive of our Lord and Saviour. Jesus stated, "By this, shall all men know that you are my disciples, if you have love one to another". St. John 13:35. How we treat each other is the litmus test and identification of membership in the family of faith. We are not to let a breakdown in a relationship continue without investigation as to the cause and ultimate resolution.

A possible breakdown in a relationship may be brought to your attention through Divine intervention. A certain person has something against you. The question now arises, what are you going to do? The directive according to scripture is to go to that person and make peace with them. It is at this point that hesitation with a number of questions begins to flood our minds. We ask, "What if you ask forgiveness and they won't forgive you?" It must be stated that we are responsible for our own actions. You went to that person who had something against you, and sought forgiveness. You went to make peace. You have discharged your responsibility. You can then return to the alter and your gift would be accepted.

When stating that you have discharged your responsibility, should positive feelings be experienced? Is it possible that you may not 'feel' that you have been forgiven? What determines if you have been forgiven? Does not feeling forgiven, have a bearing on the success of the experience? This experience, and the feeling or lack of, should not in reality, have a bearing on the success of the experience. As far as you are concerned, it was a success. You were obedient. You did what you were directed to do. This may give the impression of taking a very cold and matter-of-fact position, but in reality, this is the only position you should take. "I've done what I was told to do".

What if contact was made with the one who had something against you? Two areas of concern become very clear.

1. Before the reality of there being a rift in the relationship, the one who had something against you, continued without disruption in his life.
2. Before the reality of the situation was brought to your attention, you continued as though there was no problem or area of concern. Your situation changed when it was brought to your attention that someone had something against you. With this knowledge comes the responsibility to investigate and work towards reconciliation. Failure to follow the directive to go to that person who has something against you and is holding a grudge will heighten the rift between you and that person. There is something insidious when this situation is allowed to continue. By not going to that person, the situation becomes more serious and more in need of restitution.

The family of faith is made up of individuals with individual responsibilities. Each member of this community has been given a Divine directive to engage in relationships that will give evidence that he is a follower of Jesus Christ. This evidence is to be clear and instrumental in providing an incentive to those outside the family of faith, to investigate and consider membership in the family. There is to a marked difference in relational dynamics within the family of faith as opposed to those outside the 'family'. When this marked difference is not 'front and centre' in a relationship within the family of faith, those outside the family become disillusioned with the value of pursuing membership within the family. "Why should I join with 'that bunch' that are at each other's throats when I'm in the same position where I'm at now?" It is possible, when the Spirit of God brought the issue to your mind that He was also at work within the heart of the one holding the grudge.

The situation changed, as well, for the one who had something against you when the reality of the situation was brought to their attention. There is a definite operation of the Holy Spirit at work in this situation.

It is important to investigate the rationale and outcome of the one being asked to forgive. Aside from the one asking forgiveness, consideration has to be given to the one of whom forgiveness was asked. The comment, made by the one being asked to forgive that they would forgive, but could not/would not forget, requires clarity.

Lewis B. Smedes in his book; Forgive and Forget (Harper and Row) explores in great depth, the process and the effect of forgiving especially for the one being asked to forgive. In his book, he makes reference to the Scottish theologian H.R. MacIntosh's comment that "Forgiveness is an active process of the mind and temper of a wronged person, by means of which he abolishes a moral hindrance to fellowship with the wrongdoer, and reestablishes the freedom and happiness of friendship".
"It is to be an attitude of the mind even before you are asked to forgive". (Baker's Theological Dictionary)

Although the greatest and highest degree of onus lies with the one being asked to forgive, importance to obedience on both sides of the equation is of extreme necessity. The directive given by Jesus is extremely clear. "If we do not forgive, we will not be forgiven". Matt. 6:14, 15.
Another rendering of this verse states that if you forgive others the wrongs they have done, your heavenly Father will also forgive you; but if you do not forgive others, than

the wrongs you have done will not be forgiven by your Father. (N.E.B.)

Aside from any other consideration, the important step in the healing of a relationship is the granting of forgiveness.

Jesus stressed the importance of there not being any limitations to forgiveness. Jesus stated: " . . . . if you do not forgive your brother from your heart". Matt. 18: 35 (R.S.V.)

Granting forgiveness from the heart removes 'conditional forgiveness'. Conditional forgiveness is evident when the comment is made that 'I will forgive, but not forget'. It is no wonder that the one asking forgiveness struggles with the *feeling* of not being forgiven. It would appear the forgiveness 'supposedly' given, was insincere, and a trial period would ensue. It was given with a 'rider' or a condition. "I'll forgive him, but I'll wait and see if he will 'mess up' again. Taking this position in the process results in the erection of a wall of protection and a relationship developed at arm's length that is strained.

True forgiveness is a letting down of all barriers without any conditions or trial periods. Jesus gave the directive that if your brother comes back over and over again asking forgiveness, we are to grant forgiveness. Matthew 18:21, 22. How edifying and supportive it is when a brother or sister comes to us and seeks forgiveness and from the sincerity of our hearts, we forgive them. They may come back again and, instead of raising our eyebrows and saying within ourselves, "Here we go again", we take that brother or sister to the Lord in prayer, and get under the burden they are bearing, and ask God, by His Holy Spirit, to come-along-side to help them through their struggle. How uplifting!

So often in our dealings, we become occupied with that which will protect us. Someone has been quoted as saying; "If you do it to me the first time, shame on you. If you do it to me the second time, shame on me". We will do everything in our power to protect ourselves from any form of what we call abuse. We never want to be taken advantage of. As a result of this protectionism, we keep at arm's length anyone who keeps coming back requiring extended support. "We only have so much time you know. They have to grow up and mature". Such are the comments and positions taken many times by those within the family of faith.

The apostle Paul in his letter to the church at Colossae addressed the issue of developing and maintaining Christian relationships. "Therefore as God's chosen people, holy and beloved, clothe yourselves with compassion, kindness, humility, gentleness and patience. Bear with each other and forgive whatever grievances you may have against one another. **Forgive as the Lord forgave you.** (emphasis added) And over all these virtues put on love, which binds them all together in perfect unity". Col.3:12-14 N.I.V. The directive to forgive as we have been forgiven comes into focus in this letter written by the apostle.

Throughout Scripture, we are reminded that we are not alone in our struggles of life. The trials and times of testing we endure are not reserved for us individually, but are common to each of us. "No temptation (testing . . . added) has come your way that is too hard for flesh and blood to bear. But God can be trusted not to allow you to suffer any temptation (testing . . . added) beyond your powers of endurance. He will see to it that every temptation (testing . . . added) has a way out, so that it will never be impossible for you to bear.

II Corinthians 10:13 (Phillips).

The One we serve was tested in every way we are tested, but did not sin. Jesus Christ has been there and He knows, yes, He knows, just how much we can bear but will with the testing provide a way of escape. The way of escape is found by throwing yourself on the mercy of God.

God has no hands but our hands. He has no feet but our feet. The establishment of brotherhood/sisterhood has been entrenched in the make-up of the family of faith since its conception on the Day of Pentecost. We of the family of faith are to work at what will bring unity within the family. We are to work at being kind to each other. We are to be tenderhearted. We are to forgive each other even as God for Christ's sake has forgiven us. Ephesians 4:32.

We are directed without any degree of hesitation, to be involved with each other; to get under the burdens of life we each bear. We are to work to lift that burden from our brother or sister.

Examination of human relations within the community of faith reveals two major relational dynamics, which will add to isolation and protectionism within the family of faith unless addressed.

~~~~~~~~~~~~~~~~~~

NOTES

PERSONAL
vs.
PRIVATE

~~~~~~~~~~~~~~~

PERSONAL VS. PRIVATE

Inner conflict takes it toll when life's struggles are placed under the classification of privacy. Granted, our walk of faith is extremely personal but we are not to live our lives apart from the interaction we are to have with each other. When we regard and attempt to live our lives under the sphere of privacy, we add to the dilemma of isolation. As members of the community of faith, the mandate we have received from our heavenly Father is to stand beside each other. From the personal standpoint, we do experience personal trials and tribulation. When we are confronted by something that is beyond our degree of resiliency, what are we to do?

How often has it been that when you have been confronted with something that you have found too big to handle, you cried out to God? You asked for His help and assistance. How many times was that prayer answered by someone who came by and gave you a word of encouragement or guidance? There had been times when the person who came-along-side did not know anything about the struggle you were facing but was obedient to what was placed on their heart. Your prayer was answered.

Remember when you were in attendance at a service of worship, and the preacher felt impressed to deviate from his prepared sermon, and to speak a word given him at that moment which spoke directly to your need. How uplifted you felt. You were filled with thanksgiving and praise to God for answering prayer.

The apostle wrote to the church at Corinth stating that the Father of our Lord Jesus Christ, the all-merciful Father, the God whose consolation never fails us, ***comforts us in all our troubles, so that we in turn may be able to comfort others in any trouble of theirs and to share with them the consolation we ourselves receive from God.*** I Corinthians 1:3-4 (N.E.B.)
What tremendous support we can receive from those who have gone through what we are going through. In the community of faith, we stand beside each other to give support and encouragement with the same support and encouragement we have received when in need.

Upon review, the thought comes to mind that it certainly looks good on paper. Some would go so far as to say, "If it would only work that way". Personal experience confirms how gratifying and uplifting this whole process is. Reaching out in my time of need, I was met with help, encouragement and support so that I am able to reach out and offer the same help I received in my time of trouble, to others.

As I began to investigate the process of developing and maintaining relationships that will serve to edify, I was confronted by the reality and need for transparency and vulnerability.

Transparency has been defined as: openness, straightforwardness, clearness, obviousness. (Gage Canadian Dictionary) Within this definition, there is no 'sleight of hand'. With transparency there is absence of ambiguousness. What you see is what you get. Everything is above board.
When transparency is recognized, another reality is recognized as well. With transparency comes vulnerability.
Vulnerability is that which accessible, exposed and wide open is. (Gage Canadian Dictionary)

A vital connection exists with transparency and vulnerability. With transparency comes vulnerability. The two are intertwined to the point that it cannot be identified where each one starts in a relationship. It seems as though there is singleness of awareness. Vulnerability is the by-product of transparency.

The presence of both realities is noteworthy, but another reality has to be brought forth. It is this reality that poses a challenge when working to maintain right relationships and eliminate the isolation mentality that ensues. When you allow yourself to be vulnerable, a risk occurs that presents a challenge. I would suggest that this can present the greatest hindrance towards a healthy and open relationship. Openness in a relationship leaves you 'open'. Open to whatever may come your way. You may become the target of criticism. "Why would he tell us that?"

It is ironic that when you begin to reference a negative outcome in being transparent, that those who would criticize are the same ones who voice appreciation when they discover someone who is open. Perhaps the area in which openness was criticized 'touched a nerve', causing them to react in this manner.

It may be that the criticism stemmed from the wish they could be open, but they were overcome with jealousy. Suffice to say, when transparency does occur in a relationship, it provides a comfort zone for others who are struggling with the same challenge. A bond is formed.

Comments have often been made in appreciation for transparency. "I'm so glad you shared that. I'm going through the same thing myself". A door of communication is opened. The support and comfort you received from God when you were going through that struggle can then be shared with the brother or sister needing the same comfort and support you received. You can then come-along-side. In review of the two main ingredients in the development and maintenance of a 'good' relationship, it has to be mentioned once again, that you are responsible for your own actions. By being 'open' you may get 'shot down', but the positive outcome of the action of being open, goes beyond anything you could have imagined.

Once again, reference to the positive outcome in the revelation and observation of the two realities of transparency and vulnerability may appear extremely idealistic. Seeking to accomplish these 'targets' may seem distant. The reality of life suggests that this is what we as individuals within the family of faith desire and strive towards. This is what we are to be 'all about'.

The risk of being 'shot down' is very real. It has to be said that the fear of being shot down gives occasion to being 'closed' with walls of isolation and protection being created.

This exploration of human relations brings us back to ground zero as it relates to the basic approach to interaction. Observation of the progress and state of human interaction reveals major adjustments have to be made.

There are those in the family of faith who struggle behind walls of self-incrimination and discouragement. This is not to be.

The Scriptures are replete in addressing relationships. Our heavenly Father desired to have fellowship with us, but sin separated and disallowed that relationship. God sent His only Son Jesus to reconcile and bring us back into fellowship with Him. Through the sacrifice of Jesus on the cross of Calvary and His subsequent resurrection, fellowship is now possible. Throughout the Word of God we are directed to work at developing and maintaining right relationships with each other within the family of faith.

In the interest of clarity, maintaining a right relationship within the family of faith has to be the first priority. It is not praise worthy to give testimony of developing a right relationship with those outside the family when there are those within the family with whom you are having difficulty and have not reached closure. This may appear to be self-centered but this is the foundation and starting point in presenting a witness to those outside the family of faith. "By this shall all men know (recognize . . . added) that ye are my disciples, if you have love to one another". St. John 13:35. In reference to a previous comment, when there is conflict within the family of faith, those looking on from outside the family, are aware of this conflict and decline involvement.

It is to be understood, that this exploration of human relations is being approached from the standpoint of idealism. The standard is set very high. This is how members within the family of faith are to conduct themselves before their brothers and sisters of faith. This cannot be minimized or downplayed lest the effect of a positive witness be jeopardized.

When examination of Scripture is carried out, steps to follow the directive will be found to be very clear.

1. We are known to be followers of Jesus Christ by the love we have for each other within the family of faith. This is interactive love. It is a love that moves beyond mere oratory.

2. We are to treat each other as we would like to be treated. What has been called 'The Golden Rule' was given by Jesus. "Treat other people exactly as you would like to be treated by them—this is the essence of all true religion". Matthew 7:12 (Phillips)

When reviewing these two steps, face value would indicate simplicity. The first step is to realize and accept the fact that we are members of a family. Within this family the expectation of having and showing love for each other is to be found. The Apostle Paul's letter to the church at Corinth outlines and gives clear expression to the relational

role each member of the 'body of Christ'
(the family of faith) is to engage in.
II Corinthians 12:12-26.
The Apostle Paul in his letter to the church
at Galatia emphasized the application of
new principles for the community of faith.
He states that as we have opportunity let
us do good to all people, especially to
those who belong to the family of believers
(faith). Galatians 6:10 (N.I.V.)
In this letter, Paul outlines in detail principles
that are to be followed when interacting
with 'people' regardless of their place or
lack of place within the family of faith. He
acknowledges that the members of the
community of faith do not live in a vacuum.
They rub shoulders with other human
beings, that although others haven't chosen
to follow the Man of Galilee and become
members of the community of faith, they
are to be treated with goodness.

This approach is found throughout Scripture.
We of the family of faith, are to present
ourselves in such a way as to entice others
to come and follow the One in whom we
have placed our trust. Jesus said, "And you,
like the lamp, must shed light among your
fellows, so that, when they see the good
you do, they may give praise to your Father
in heaven". Matthew 5:16 (N.I.V.)

To whom are we to do good in order that praise will be given to our Father in heaven? We are to give this good to all people.

It is how we treat each other as members of the community of faith that will serve to be the means of attracting others to become followers of Jesus Christ.

In review of a possible outcome of this approach, someone could be overheard saying; "Look how they treat each other who are supposed to be their spiritual brother and sister. They treat people outside their group better than they treat each other". The effect this would have on bringing others into the family of faith would be that they would not wish to become involved.

In our society, and especially due to the spiritual foundation on which our society has been built, the high standard of interaction found in Scripture, has been well documented. It is for this reason that people looking on have been so taken aback when these expectations are not met by those within the family of faith.
On the other hand, if the observation was made that those within the family

of faith were seen treating each other with noticeable kindness and regard, the following comment could be made. "They go out of their way to treat each other with kindness and respect. They can't do enough to help each other". This would result in others coming into the family of faith. It has been written that many early converts to the faith, such as Justin Martyr, were first attracted by the love they saw among believers. (Eerdman's Handbook to the History of Christianity)

When making a comparison of the two outcomes of the treatment of each other, the conclusion would be reached, that the second outcome would lend itself to entice membership into the family or, at the least, investigation into the family of faith. This would be based on what was seen in the carrying out of relationships.

Once again, it has to be said, that the pursuit of this high level of relational interaction with the desired outcome, certainly appears difficult to accomplish. The standard seems so high.

Even though the difficulty would be recognized, we would be remiss if we were to regard the difficulty beyond our responsibility to pursue. As members of the community of faith, we have a tremendous source of help and assistance. The ministry of the Holy Spirit will work in us, to fulfill the will of God as it relates to presenting this enticing appeal to those outside the family of faith.

The breakdown of the isolation mentality between members of the family of faith will provide a safe haven of support and acceptance to those who are seeking comfort.

~~~~~~~~~~~~~~~

NOTES

EXCLUSIVENESS
VS.
INCLUSIVENESS

~~~~~~~~~~~~~~~~

EXCLUSIVENESS
VS.
INCLUSIVENESS

The apostle Paul gives attention to a state of exclusiveness that existed in the church at Corinth. There was a sense of elitism that separated those that felt they were of greater importance in the body of Christ, from those who regarded themselves insignificant. Paul stated very clearly that there was/is not to be any division in the body. Everyone was/is to be regarded and treated equally. " . . . . all the members of that one body, being many, are one body; so also is Christ: II Corinthians 12:12.

The position of inclusiveness shines forth very clearly in Scripture and removes any thought of exclusiveness based on external differences. The acceptance of the redemptive sacrifice of Jesus on the cross brought ***all believers*** into fellowship with each other. No longer is there to be exclusiveness to any group or person based on ethnicity or heritage. We are one in Christ and each is a brother or sister within the family of faith. When we allow this truth to grip our heart with 'bull-dog tenacity' it will serve to revolutionize the approach we take towards a brother or sister in need, regardless of any and every external distinction. The ground is level at the foot of the cross. The cross of Jesus Christ provides a positive outcome to every relationship when the power of the cross is accepted and acted on by faith. The cross unites and makes us one in Christ Jesus.

The state of exclusiveness that was found in the church at Corinth is found in the family of faith even today. This exclusiveness can be compared to the inter-relational struggle referenced at the beginning of this effort. Even though you do not find the use of a hyphen to identify denominational preference, the outcome is the same as those who use the hyphenated usage for ethnical identification. Within the family of faith, we can refer to this as denominational distinction. Someone may be identified as Baptist-Christian, or Pentecostal-Christian, etc.

The result of this elitism is isolation from those that are 'not of my group'. This has the effect of protectionism and is very divisive.

A young fellow, who graduated after completing his theological education, was

consumed with the compulsion to be in
pulpit ministry. Two years following his
graduation, an appointment was made with
a senior pastor responsible for submitting
names of possible candidates for pulpit
ministry. Following the interview, this
young fellow left the office of this pastor,
steaming. The pastor did not roll out the
'red carpet' and extol the outstanding
qualities of this young would-be pastor.
There was no heightened awareness or
verbal commendations this young fellow
felt he deserved. This immature yet sincere
young man, pushed every button he
could find to 'push his way' into pulpit
ministry.
His efforts did meet with success. He was
assigned to pastor a church and began an
education that could only be described as
a training period under the guidance and
direction of the Holy Spirit.

At the conclusion of nine months of giving
spiritual leadership to this congregation,
the decision was made to leave the
pastorate, and enter the evangelistic field.
Prior to leaving this particular situation,
he came in contact with a couple in need
of someone to come-along-side to offer
encouragement and support. This couple
was not of the same 'group' as this young

man, and because of this they did not receive the help and encouragement they were seeking.

This young man with his wife and son began evangelistic ministry holding meetings in different churches every one to two weeks. His wife and son traveled for one year before a decision was made for this young evangelist to travel alone. An apartment was secured for his family and the young man traveled for three years on the evangelistic field and experienced God's blessing, as the Word of God was honoured.

Even though God displayed mercy and grace, it became evident there was an embedded attitude which raised its ugly head from time to time that brought an indictment to the witness of the family of faith.

Following three years of full-time evangelistic ministry, during which time I became ordained within my particular denomination, I left the 'field' and continued to provide pulpit supply whenever possible. I secured employment working 8-4 Monday to Friday to provide for my family.

The same attitude I had displayed during my interview and the 9 years following proved to be detrimental to the positive image given in Scripture, as it relates to developing and exhibiting proper relationships within the family of faith. This also had the effect of hindering me from giving the support to others as required as a member of the family of faith.

It was at this point nine years following that interview, that God had enough of this display of negativism. For 9 years, I continued to display this non-Christian attitude towards those outside 'my group'. When I met a member of the family of faith, instead of seeking to build them up and discover means of supporting them, I would seek to win them over to 'my camp'.

This had gone on for 9 years until August 12, 1972 at 2:00 a.m. when I was wakened from sleep. As I walked into the living-room of our apartment, I was compelled to prostrate myself on the floor. While on the floor God pulled back the curtain of my heart, and began to show me what He had to deal with. It was not a pretty sight. Self-importance, arrogance, pride, and a host of other revelations revealed how sickening this sight was. I became broken as God began to burn all that 'stuff' out of my heart. I was broken that morning as I have never been broken before. I remember this experience as though it happened this morning. I have never forgotten that encounter.

Even though I was devastated during the encounter that morning, God did not put His size 15 EEEEE foot on me and push me down into a ditch. He stood with His arms outstretched telling me that even though He had all this to deal with, He loved me with an everlasting love.

As I recall this event 36 years later, I find myself so ashamed and so very repentant, but determined to maintain what I was instructed to do that morning.

From that time forward, God has opened vast areas of ministry into every part of the body of Christ. When meeting someone who is a member of the family of faith, their particular denominational preference does not have an effect on our conversation. I have learned and continue to learn and accept the fact that I am to make it my aim to be one in the Spirit, and that I would inevitably be at peace with one another. Ephesians 4:3 (Phillips)

Someone made reference to denominational preference in a scenario that I have taken as my own. This fellow died, and went to heaven. At the gate of heaven, Peter had been given the responsibility to welcome the newcomers. On this particular occasion, an angel was standing beside Peter with a pair of scissors in his hand. The fellow was welcomed at the gate, and Peter introduced himself and stated he was there to welcome him. The fellow said he was aware of Peter's responsibility to welcome him into heaven, but why was the angel standing there? Peter went on to say, that yes, he was to welcome the fellow into heaven, and that the angel was there to snip off the denominational tag.

This incident spoke to my heart as it described how much value I had placed on denominational preference. If you were not of 'my camp', the challenge to win you over became my goal.

The result of this pre-occupation caused harm and placed a stumbling block in the path of others looking on. Thank God for His love and mercy. Over time, I have had the opportunity to minister in churches of every denominational stripe as well as serving in a Christian-based trans-denominational community service organization for a number of years.

~~~~~~~~~~~~~~~~~~~~~~

NOTES

REFLECTION OF OUR
TREATMENT OF
OTHERS

~~~~~~~~~~~~~~~~

REFLECTION IN OUR TREATMENT OF OTHERS

On a day to day basis, as a member of the family of faith, we are expected to go out of our way to treat each other in the same way we want to be treated. Once again, at face value, it would indicate simplicity. Is it really *that* hard to treat someone else the same way we would want to be treated? If we could only distance ourselves from situations that leave us struggling to retain our 'I've got it all together posture', it would certainly make the journey of faith so much easier . . . so we think. When we go out of our way to come-along-side someone in need of encouragement and support, we take personal inventory to determine how we can be of help.

As we interact, the request to lend support is made. This may mean the giving of time. It may mean holding them in prayer. It will definitely mean giving them the same comfort we received in our time of need. We go beyond ourselves and become 'attached' to that brother or sister in their time of need.

Please understand. We cannot ignore the reality of personal personalities that will come to play in this process. Occasions will arise when we will be misunderstood. We may be criticized in what we say. This will at times come from those to whom we are 'attached'. In these circumstances, what are we to do?

Jesus said that in our time of prayer, when it has been brought to our attention that someone has something against us, we are to go to them and be reconciled to them. Matthew 5:24. One translation translates reconciled; to make your peace with them. (Phillips)

The apostle Paul in his letter to the church at Rome gives the directive that if it is possible, **as far as it depends on you,** live at peace with everyone.
Romans 12:18 (N.I.V.)
Another rendering of this verse states, As far as your responsibility goes. (Phillip)
Jesus gave the directive that, when it was not possible to resolve a relational situation after you have gone to a brother, there are steps to follow. Matthew 18:15-17.

These steps include a fleshing out of the situation with 'all cards' placed on the table of exposure. Included in these steps is the role of the church. Jesus stressed the importance of not leaving any stone unturned in dealing with an unresolved issue.

1. You are to go to the brother alone. Just the two of you are to meet.

2. If the issue is not resolves, you are to return with one or two other brothers.

3. If the situation continues in the impasse, the matter is to be brought to the leadership of the church.

4. If again the situation is not resolved, he is to be regarded as an outsider.

It is of interest to note the directive and steps Jesus gave in the event resolution could not occur. The outcome is certainly revealing as to the condition in the heart of the one who would not listen.

This outcome brings us back to the Sermon on the Mount and the directive Jesus gave to address hidden difficulties that were brought to light. Once again action is to be taken to address relational deterioration.

When taking into account situations that exist in many sectors of the family, we are brought up short with the question as to why we are allowing this deterioration between members to continue.

There will certainly be a response following each of the steps Jesus gave to address the situation. A more accepting outcome would result if the issue was resolved following the first step. When the issue was brought to the attention of the one who was 'holding a grudge', and resolution followed, relationship was reaffirmed. This would certainly be the ideal. Unfortunately, resolution does not always follow the initial encounter.

When resolution has not taken place following that first encounter and the second step is followed, a sense of defensiveness can occur. "They are ganging up on me, I have to defend myself". There can be as many as three individuals facing the one who would not listen. It can be intimidating and challenging.

When the second step has to be implemented, a more accurate state of the relationship is revealed and ultimately what is really taking place within the heart of the one who would not listen is shown. This second step is indicative of the fact that the granting of forgiveness has not been extended.

The third step in the directive Jesus gave to address this situation, requires close examination. There is general knowledge and experience regarding how some churches deal with relational issues. Other issues come to bear when relational issues have to be dealt with. There are times when the decision to address or not address such issues, are determined by either the position and /or financial influence of the person being approached.

As well, departure has, on occasion, followed when the individual has been approached by the leadership of the church in an effort to resolve the issue. Concern follows when an individual leaves a church under any circumstance, but when departure is the outcome of being addressed by the leadership concerning a matter that has not been resolved, a greater level of concern develops.

It has been said that no one is chained to a church, and that departure can be justified for any number of legitimate reasons. The *reason* for the departure is the concern for leaving a particular church. If departure is for the wrong reason, that unresolved issue will follow and go before them to the next location.

The following step is extremely unfortunate. Jesus stated that if this fourth step has to be taken, the party that will not listen and neglects the directive of the church, is to be regarded as an outsider. Paul in his letter to the church at Rome follows the directive given by Jesus. In Romans 16:17, he directs the church to mark them which cause divisions and offences contrary to the doctrine which they had learned, and to keep away from them. Again, in his letter to the church at Thessalonica, he instructs them to withdraw from every brother (sister . . . added) that walks disorderly and not after the tradition they had received. II Thessalonians 3:6-15.

Paul admonishes in his letter, not to count them as an enemy, but to warn them as a brother. (sister . . . added)

Having read Paul's instruction in his letter to the Thessalonians, do we not find ourselves faced with the challenge to give support to this member of the family? Paul stated that we are not to treat them as an enemy, but warn them as a brother/sister. What would this warning entail? Included is the instruction to disassociate from the one who has engaged in a disorderly fashion. There is to be distance created between those who are spiritual from those that have been overtaken by a fault.

With this directive, is there room for any redemptive work in the life and heart of the one overtaken by a fault? When reviewing steps to take in this exploration of human relations, should there not be some effort to 'come-along-side' that one who has been overtaken by a fault? Jesus stated, that the one who would not listen to the instructions given, was to be regarded as an outsider. During the ministry of Jesus, those who were regarded as outsiders were brought into fellowship.

Matthew had become a tax gatherer for the Romans. This position was deeply dishonourable. Matthew equates publicans with harlots in his gospel. Jesus equates those that will not listen, to the dishonourable role of a publican. Matthew became a disciple of Jesus. He left the receipt of custom and opened his home to Jesus, and gave a great feast inviting many publicans to come and hear Jesus.

There is a definite work of the Holy Spirit in effect to bring one to faith in Jesus. There is a definite work of the Holy Spirit in establishing a right on-going relationship with Jesus. It is the Spirit of God that burns up the dross and impurities that come between the soul and the Saviour. The cry outlined in a Gospel song, states there is nothing preventing the least of His favour. It continues keeping the way clear and let nothing come between.

The need for support becomes crucial for the one who has been overtaken by a fault. God will, by His Holy Spirit, bring to the attention of a member of the family of faith the need for prayer. Even though there has been disobedience to the directive to resolve and work to correct this situation, the love of God continues to be available for this one in need of restoration.

Recognition of the need for Divine intervention should cause members of the family of faith, to engage in prayer and supplication on behalf of this brother or sister in need. Emphasis on and acceptance of the power of prayer, has to be taken into account in this situation. Whatever thoughts are entertained, the reality remains; this is a member of the family of faith who is in need of prayer.

When examining this exploration, positive interaction cannot be ignored. This interaction includes acceptance and the giving of the benefit of a doubt. It goes without saying that this aspect of interaction has become obscure due to heightened negativism and suspicion in our present society.

~~~~~~~~~~~~~~~~~~~~

NOTES

COMING
INTO
VIEW

~~~~~~~~~~~~~~~~

COMING INTO VIEW

Throughout this exploration of human relations, many questions have been brought forward. Questions that have evolved through the examination of practical situations we face on our journey of life. The conclusion that is reached in light of our response to many of the questions raised is that this is an on-going process. Each (serious) situation we face requires examination. How am I to relate to my brother or sister of faith in my time of need? Can I pull back the curtain and expose the depth of the struggle I am personally facing? How do I know I can trust that person to whom I have revealed my struggle? This position and ensuing questions are very prevalent in the natural realm.

Seeking the direction and assistance of the Holy Spirit will provide positive transition from the natural realm to the realm of relationships that go above and beyond what we have conjured within our own minds.

It has been stated earlier that we are each responsible for our own actions. I am not responsible to give an account of how you conducted yourself in a relationship. On the other hand, you are not responsible for my actions. We will each stand to give account of our own actions on that day of accountability.

Having said that, when I look in the mirror, I have to ask the one looking back at me, "What are you going to do in light of the expectations given as a member of the community of faith?" I am the only one who can make the determination to either follow the directive or disregard what has been written.

There are those we come in contact with on a day to day basis that struggle with issues of life. The struggle may take place behind walls of isolation and protection. The struggle may be hidden by an insincere smile or false statement that everything is fine.

You may find yourself in a state of turmoil, needing someone to come-along-side in your hour of need. All of this and more indicate a need to interact and become 'attached'.

I was reminded of the words of a chorus. Lord, lay some soul upon my heart, and love that soul through me. And may I ever do my part, to win that soul for Thee. I would suggest a slight change to those words. And may I ever do my part, to *support that soul* for Thee.

Isolation, separation and personal exclusion destroys the supportive portrayal of the family of faith, in the eyes of those outside the family. The usage of the hyphen, even though hidden as it relates to relations within the community of faith, can be very divisive.

"As a prisoner for the Lord, then, I urge you to live a life worthy of the calling you have received. Be completely humble and gentle; be patient, bearing with one another in love. Make every effort to keep the unity of the Spirit through the bond of peace. There is one body and one Spirit—just as you were called to one hope when you were called—one Lord, one faith, one baptism; one God and Father of all, who is over all and through all and in all". Ephesians 4:1-6 (N.I.V.)

~~~~~~~~~~~~~~~~~~~~

NOTES

www.ingramcontent.com/pod-product-compliance
Lightning Source LLC
Chambersburg PA
CBHW021229280526
45784CB00005B/2031